BANGLADESH: HUMAN RIGHTS

EXECUTIVE SUMMARY

Bangladesh is a parliamentary democracy. Prime Minister Sheikh Hasina led the Awami League (AL) to victory in the 2008 parliamentary elections, which international and domestic observers considered free and fair, although with isolated irregularities and sporadic violence. Authorities failed at times to maintain effective control over security forces. Security forces reportedly committed human rights abuses.

The most significant human rights problems were arbitrary arrests, regulation of online speech, and poor working conditions and labor rights.

Other human rights problems included extrajudicial killings, arbitrary detentions, weak judicial capacity, and lengthy pretrial detentions. Authorities infringed on citizens' privacy rights. Politically motivated violence and pervasive official corruption remained serious problems. Some nongovernmental organizations (NGOs) faced legal and informal restrictions on their activities. Women suffered from unequal treatment. Many children were compelled to work, particularly in the informal sector, due either to economic necessity or in some instances trafficking. Discrimination against persons with disabilities was a problem, especially for children seeking admittance to public school. Instances of societal violence against religious and ethnic minorities persisted, although many government and civil society leaders claimed these acts had political or economic motivations and should not be attributed wholly to religious beliefs or affiliations. Child marriage of girls was a problem. Discrimination against persons based on their sexual orientation continued.

Official corruption and related impunity remained problems. Weak regard for the rule of law not only enabled individuals, including government officials, to commit human rights violations with impunity but also prevented citizens from claiming their rights. As in recent years, the government did not take comprehensive measures to investigate and prosecute cases of security force abuse and killing.

Section 1. Respect for the Integrity of the Person, Including Freedom from:

a. Arbitrary or Unlawful Deprivation of Life

The constitution provides for the rights to life and personal liberty; however, the media and local and international human rights organizations reported that the government or its agents committed arbitrary or unlawful killings.

The government neither released statistics on total killings by security personnel nor took comprehensive measures to investigate cases, despite previous statements by high-ranking officials that the government would show "zero tolerance" and fully investigate all extrajudicial killings by security forces. According to the media and local human rights organizations, no case resulted in criminal punishment during the year and, in the few instances in which the government brought charges, those found guilty generally received only administrative punishment. Some members of the security forces acted with impunity. The government formed an internal inquiries cell within the paramilitary Rapid Action Battalion (RAB) to investigate cases of human rights abuses, but during the year there was no information disclosed on any prosecutions for suspected killings by RAB officers.

The legal aid and human rights NGO Ain o Salish Kendra (ASK) reported that during the first nine months of the year, security forces, including the RAB, committed an estimated total of 146 killings. The deaths occurred during raids, arrests, and other law-enforcement operations. The government often described these deaths as "crossfire killings," "gunfights," or "encounter killings," terms used to characterize exchanges of gunfire between RAB or police units and criminal gangs. Throughout 2012 there were an estimated 70 extrajudicial killings.

On February 24, according to local media reports, police opened fire on demonstrators in Singair, Manikganj, and killed five persons during a nationwide general strike (hartal). Local residents told *The Daily Star* newspaper that the victims were apolitical and not strike participants. Police stated that they fired approximately 200 gunshots and teargas shells to bring the situation under control but resorted to deadly force after hartal supporters attacked police with sticks and rocks. The dead included farmer Alamgir Hossain, trader Nasir Ahmed, and students Nazimuddin Mollah and Shah Alam.

According to ASK, 189 persons were killed and 10,048 injured in political violence from January through September. There were 135 incidents of intraparty violence within the ruling AL, resulting in the deaths of 15 persons and the injury of 1,738 others. In the opposition Bangladesh Nationalist Party (BNP), there were 75 incidents of internal violence, which killed six individuals and injured 945.

These incidents were often linked to criminal activities rather than to political motives. Incidents of nonlethal, politically motivated violence also occurred.

In December the Dhaka High Court handed down death sentencesto eight persons and life imprisonment to 13 others for their involvement in the December 2012 death of Biswajit Das, an apolitical Hindu man, who was stabbed and killed during a blockade that turned violent.

b. Disappearance

Disappearances and kidnappings, some committed by security services such as the RAB and the Criminal Investigative Division, continued during the year. According to prominent local human rights NGO Odhikar, from January through September, there were 14 disappearances allegedly involving security personnel, compared with 24 in 2012. Odhikar claimed RAB involvement in two of those disappearances. For the same period, ASK estimated there were 33 disappearances.

According to Odhikar, on January 25, the RAB abducted Mohammad Ali Mohabbat, a leader of the National Communist Party, in Kumarkhali, Kushtia. Family members of Mohammad Anwarul Islam, who was involved in the local student wing of Jamaat-e-Islami (Jamaat), an Islamist party, claimed they have not heard from Islam since the RAB arrested him on April 5. The men's whereabouts were unknown at year's end.

On May 15, International Crimes Tribunal (ICT) witness Shukoranjan Bali told the local daily *The New Age* that plainclothes police abducted him from the ICT court in November 2012. The prosecution denied the abduction took place, despite eyewitness testimony, and did not conduct an investigation. Bali stated the government held him in custody for several weeks prior to forcing him to cross the border to India illegally. He remained in a Kolkata jail at year's end.

c. Torture and Other Cruel, Inhuman, or Degrading Treatment or Punishment

Although the constitution and law prohibit torture and other cruel, inhuman, or degrading treatment or punishment, local and international human rights organizations and the media reported security forces, including the RAB and police, employed torture and physical and psychological abuse during arrests and interrogations. Security forces used threats, beatings, and electric shock.

According to Odhikar, security forces tortured 23 persons, killing eight. The government rarely charged, convicted, or punished those responsible.

Parliament passed the Torture and Custodial Death (Prevention) Act on October 24. The act criminalizes torture in custody and stipulates a minimum punishment of life imprisonment with fines for members of law enforcement and security agencies or government officials for causing or committing death, torture, and inhuman treatment of detainees in custody. The act also makes an offender liable for paying the victom's family 200,000 taka ($2,500) in compensation. Moreover, the act states that officials guilty of torture, inhuman treatment, or death in custody may not justify their acts by citing exceptional circumstances, including state of war, internal political stability, state of emergency, or an order from a superior officer or public authority.

The law contains provisions allowing a magistrate to place a suspect in interrogative custody, known as remand, during which questioning of the suspect can take place without a lawyer present. The government made efforts to limit remand because of instances of abuse during remand.

On March 31, following several weeks of clashes with police, authorities arrested Jamaat's student wing president, Delwar Hossain, on charges of assaulting police and setting off homemade explosive devices. The court placed him in remand for 45 days, extending the initial 14-day period on four occasions. Hossain's mother stated authorities did not disclose her son's location during the remand period. Hossain appeared before the court in ankle braces, claiming he was unable to walk because of harsh custodial treatment (see also section 2.a.).

According to Odhikar, there were six recorded incidents of rape and sexual abuse by members of law enforcement agencies. Three victims were under age 17. For example, on June 8, Subinspector Zahidul Islam of Sirajdikhan Police Station in Munshiganj raped a female student of Rajdiya Abhoy Pilot High School. The family filed a case against Islam, who was suspended and arrested.

Prison and Detention Center Conditions

Prison conditions remained harsh and at times life threatening due to overcrowding, inadequate facilities, and lack of proper sanitation. Odhikar stated that these conditions contributed to custodial deaths.

According to Odhikar 46 persons died in prison through September, compared with 63 in 2012. ASK estimated 54 prison deaths occurred as of September 30.

Physical Conditions: Media and human rights observers reported the prison population as of October to be 69,968 prisoners in a system designed to hold 33,824 in 68 jails throughout the country. According to *The Independent* (an English language daily), 20,860 inmates were in pretrial detention or undergoing trial. Authorities often incarcerated pretrial detainees with convicted prisoners.

Due to overcrowding, prisoners slept in shifts and did not have adequate toilet facilities. All prisoners have the right to medical care and water. Human rights organizations and the media stated that some prisoners did not enjoy these rights. Water available in prisons was comparable with water available in the rest of the country, which was often not potable.

Conditions in prisons and often within the same prison complex varied widely because authorities lodged some prisoners in areas subject to high temperatures, poor ventilation, and overcrowding. The law allows persons with certain educational and social standing to serve their jail sentences in "divisional" custody, which features better conditions, including increased family visitation rights and access to household staff.

While the law requires holding juveniles separately from adults, many juveniles were incarcerated with adults. Children were sometimes imprisoned (occasionally with their mothers) despite laws and court decisions prohibiting the imprisonment of minors.

Authorities routinely housed female prisoners separately from men. Although the law prohibits women in "safe custody" (usually victims of rape, trafficking, and domestic violence) from being housed with criminals, officials did not always provide separate facilities.

Administration: Prison recordkeeping was adequate. Prison officials allowed prisoners to submit uncensored complaints and occasionally investigated such complaints. Authorities did not use alternatives to sentencing for nonviolent offenders, and prison ombudsmen were not available to prisoners. Authorities permitted religious observance for prisoners.

Independent Monitoring: The government did not permit prison visits by the International Committee of the Red Cross or any other independent human rights monitors. The government allowed the Bangladesh Red Crescent Society to visit foreign detainees. Government-appointed committees composed of prominent private citizens in each prison locality monitored prisons monthly but did not publicly release their findings. District judges occasionally visited prisons.

d. Arbitrary Arrest or Detention

The constitution prohibits arbitrary arrest and detention, but the law permits authorities to arrest and detain persons suspected of criminal activity without an order from a magistrate or a warrant. The government increased the number of offenses ineligible for bail (see section 2.a.).

On March 11, police raided the opposition BNP's central office and arrested more than 150 party officials during a BNP rally. Police claimed they found Molotov cocktails and bomb-making materials inside the BNP office. BNP leaders alleged the police claim was baseless and a cover to justify the office raid and party leaders' arrest. Authorities charged BNP Acting Secretary General Mirza Fakhrul Alamgir with 52 criminal counts and detained him for 91 days. Alamgir faced trial in 15 cases at year's end.

Legal experts and human rights activists criticized the use of mobile courts headed by magistrates during nationwide strikes called by the opposition party. Mobile courts immediately prosecuted persons alleged to have supported the strikes and rendered verdicts that often included prison terms.

Role of the Police and Security Apparatus

Police, who fall under the jurisdiction of the Ministry of Home Affairs (MHA), have a mandate to maintain internal security and law and order. The army, organized under the Prime Minister's Office, is responsible for external security, but it can be called to help with a variety of domestic security responsibilities when required to, "in aid to civil authority." The army and MHA security forces maintain a significant presence in the Chittagong Hills Tracts (CHT) to monitor the 1997 CHT Peace Accord.

Civilian authorities maintained effective control over the armed forces, and the government has mechanisms to investigate and punish abuse and corruption. These mechanisms were not regularly employed, however. The government took steps to improve police professionalism, discipline, training, and responsiveness and to reduce corruption. For example, a 20-officer internal affairs unit established within the RAB in 2011 received two allegations of abuse; it dismissed one and was taking action on the other at year's end. Police incorporated instruction on the use of force into their basic training as part of a campaign to implement community-based policing.

Despite such efforts security forces, including the RAB, continued to commit abuses with impunity. Plaintiffs were reluctant to accuse police in criminal cases due to lengthy trial procedures and fear of retribution. Reluctance to bring charges against police also perpetuated a climate of impunity.

Security forces failed to prevent societal violence (see section 6).

Arrest Procedures and Treatment of Detainees

The government or a district magistrate may order a person detained for 30 days to prevent the commission of an act that could threaten national security; however, authorities sometimes held detainees for longer periods. A magistrate must inform a detainee of the grounds for detention within 15 days, and regulations require an advisory board to examine the detainee's case after four months. Detainees have the right to appeal.

There is a functioning bail system in the regular courts. Authorities granted criminal detainees charged with crimes access to attorneys. The government sometimes provided detainees with state-funded defense attorneys. The few legal aid programs for detainees that existed were underfunded. Authorities generally permitted defense lawyers to meet with their clients after formal charges were filed in the courts, which in some cases occurred weeks or months after the initial arrest.

Arbitrary Arrest: Arbitrary arrests occurred, usually in conjunction with political demonstrations, and the government held persons in detention without specific charges, sometimes in an attempt to collect information about other suspects. For example, on November 8, police arrested opposition standing committee members M. K. Anwar, Rafiqul Islam Miah, Moudud Ahmed, Abdul Awal Mintoo, and Shimul Biswas. Police claimed they were responsible for instigating violence in political demonstrations, including the attempted killing of police.

Pretrial Detention: Arbitrary and lengthy pretrial detention continued to be a problem due to bureaucratic inefficiencies, limited resources, lax enforcement of pretrial rules, and corruption. An estimated two million civil and criminal cases were pending. In some cases the length of pretrial detention equaled or exceeded the sentence for the alleged crime. During the year the ICT indicted, tried, and began rendering verdicts for defendants, some of whom had been held in pretrial detention throughout 2012.

e. Denial of Fair Public Trial

The law provides for an independent judiciary; however, a provision of the constitution that accords the executive branch authority over judicial appointments of lower courts and compensation for judicial officials could undermine full judicial independence.

Corruption and a substantial backlog of cases hindered the court system, and extended continuances effectively prevented many defendants from obtaining fair trials due to witness tampering, victim intimidation, and missing evidence. Human rights observers stated that magistrates, attorneys, and court officials demanded bribes from defendants in many cases filed during the year.

Despite international concerns expressed by the UN and other bodies surrounding the process leading up to this execution, on December 12, prison authorities executed Abdul Quader Mollah, whom the ICT had previously convicted and sentenced to death for war crimes committed during the country's 1971 war of independence. The ICT had initially sentenced Mollah to life in prison on February 12. In response to continuing public protests demanding the death penalty, however, parliament enacted amendments to the ICT law on February 18 that allowed the prosecution to appeal the sentence. On September 17, the Supreme Court Appellate Division sentenced Mollah to death following an appeal of the earlier sentence. On December 8, the court issued a death warrant but stayed the execution order on December 10 to allow the defense to file a review petition. The court accepted Mollah's right to file the review petition on December 12 but then ruled against defense arguments. The attorney general and the minister of state of law claimed that the jail code, which provides a 21-day waiting period between a death warrant and an execution, did not apply to ICT cases.

On August 16, the NGO Human Rights Watch (HRW) called the ICT's trial of Ghulam Azam unfair due to allegations of collusion and bias among prosecutors and judges, failure to take steps to protect defense witnesses, changes in the trial court panel, and lack of evidence to establish guilt beyond a reasonable doubt (see section 5).

Trial Procedures

The law provides for the right to a fair trial, but the judiciary did not always protect this right due to corruption and weak human and institutional capacities. Judges received a salary increase on June 2, with base pay set from 29,200 taka ($365) to 39,600 taka ($495) per month, depending on qualifications. Prosecutors' low monthly retainer of 3,000 taka ($37.50) plus 200 taka ($2.50) per hour in court meant some were willing to accept bribes to influence the outcome of a case. Defendants are presumed innocent and have the rights to appeal and see the government's evidence. Defendants have the right to be informed promptly and in detail of the charges against them. The Speedy Trial Act prevented undue delay of proceedings for certain offenses, such as murder, sexual assault, and robbery. Judges rather than juries decide cases, and trials are public. Indigent defendants have the right to a public defender. Defendants also have adequate time to prepare a defense; adjournments are one factor that contributed to the backlog of cases. Accused persons have the rights to be represented by counsel, review accusatory material, call and question witnesses, and appeal verdicts. The government, however, frequently did not respect these rights.

The courts used mass trials to prosecute and convict members of the Bangladesh Rifles accused of participating in a 2009 mutiny. A criminal court handed down verdicts on November 5 for 847 defendants. The court convicted 152 of murder and sentenced them to death. Others received long jail sentences for conspiracy, looting, and arson.

Political Prisoners and Detainees

While political affiliation was sometimes a factor in the arrest and prosecution of members of the opposition parties, the government did not prosecute individuals solely for political reasons.

Civil Judicial Procedures and Remedies

Individuals and organizations may seek administrative and judicial remedies for human rights violations; however, the civil court system was slow and cumbersome, deterring many from filing complaints. The government did not interfere with civil judicial procedures. Corruption and outside influence were problems in the civil judicial system. Alternative dispute resolution for civil cases allowed citizens to present their cases for mediation. According to government sources, the wider use of mediation in civil cases accelerated the administration of justice, but there was no assessment of its fairness or impartiality.

Property Restitution

The government did not take action to compensate individuals, primarily Hindus, who lost their land under the 1974 Vested Property Act, despite a change to the law in 2001 requiring the return of the land (see section 2.d.).

f. Arbitrary Interference with Privacy, Family, Home, or Correspondence

The law does not prohibit arbitrary interference with private correspondence; rather, intelligence and law enforcement agencies may monitor private communications with the permission of the chief executive of the MHA. Police rarely obtained warrants as required, and authorities did not punish officers who violated these procedures. Human rights organizations alleged that the Special Branch of police, the National Security Intelligence (NSI), and the Directorate General of Forces Intelligence (DGFI) employed informers to conduct surveillance and report on citizens perceived to be critical of the government. The government also routinely conducted surveillance on opposition politicians. Human rights organizations and news outlets reported that police sometimes entered private homes without obtaining proper authorization.

Section 2. Respect for Civil Liberties, Including:

a. Freedom of Speech and Press

The constitution provides for these rights, but the government sometimes failed to respect freedom of speech and press. There were some limitations on freedom of speech; perceived misrepresentations or "defamations" of Islam sometimes garnered condemnation. Some journalists self-censored their criticisms of the government due to fear of harassment and reprisal.

Freedom of Speech: The constitution equates criticism of the constitution with sedition. Punishment for sedition ranges from three years' to life imprisonment. During the year the courts did not sentence anyone under these laws. The law limits hate speech but does not define clearly what constitutes hate speech, leaving the government with broad powers of interpretation. The government can restrict speech that is deemed to be against the security of the state; against friendly relations with foreign states; and against public order, decency, or morality or that constitutes contempt of court, defamation, or incitement to an offense.

Press Freedoms: The independent media were active and expressed a wide variety of views; however, the media that criticized the government sometimes experienced negative government pressure.

The government owned one radio station and one television station. The law mandates that the Bangladesh public television station (BTV) remain the country's only terrestrial (nonsatellite) broadcast channel. An estimated 60 percent of the population did not have access to private satellite channels, and surveys indicated that almost 80 percent of citizens received their information from television. The BTV broadcast parliamentary sessions and government programming but rarely broadcast opposition views. Cable operators generally functioned without government interference. The government required all private stations to broadcast, without charge, selected government news programs and speeches by the prime minister.

Violence and Harassment: Police subjected journalists to physical attack, harassment, and intimidation. According to Odhikar, while no journalists were killed, 144 were attacked or threatened from January through August. According to ASK, two journalists were killed, 39 were attacked or threatened by security forces, and another 234 were attacked or threatened by political parties, government officials, or criminals during the same nine-month period.

On January 14, unknown attackers stabbed blogger Asif Mohiuddin, who writes on human rights and is a founding member of the Bangladesh Online Activist Network. On February 15, unknown attackers killed blogger Ahmed Rajib Haider. Prior to his death, Haider wrote about the Shabagh movement, in which protesters called for the death penalty for ICT defendants. Police arrested one suspect on August 14 but, at year's end, had not filed charges with the court to commence a trial.

On July 20, AL Member of Parliament Golam Maula Rony assaulted Imtiaz Momin and Mohsin Mukul, two journalists investigating a corruption allegation against Rony. Mukul's camera caught the attack on film, and it was subsequently broadcast widely. On July 21, Independent Television sued Rony, whom police charged with assault and arrested on July 24. Authorities released him on bail September 10 while the case continued at year's end.

Police have not made arrests in the February 2012 killings of Sagar Sarwar, news editor of private-channel Maasranga Television, and his wife, Meherun Runi, a reporter for private-channel ATN Bangla.

<u>Censorship or Content Restrictions</u>: The government indirectly censored the media through threats and harassment. According to journalists, on multiple occasions government officials asked privately owned television channels not to broadcast the opposition's activities and statements. On February 14, the government banned print and broadcast media outlets associated with the opposition--including Amar Desh, Dinkaal, Sangram, Diganta Television, and Islamic Television--from covering any AL events.

On May 6, the Bangladesh Telecommunication and Radio Commission (BTRC) stopped all transmission of Diganta Television and Islamic Television during the two stations' live broadcasts of the Hefazat rally in the Mohtijeel area of Dhaka (see section 2.b.). Employees of both stations who were in their offices on May 6 reported that officials gave no formal notice or documentation to justify their actions. Both stations remained closed at year's end.

According to some journalists and human rights NGOs, journalists engaged in self-censorship due to fear of government retribution. Although public criticism of the government was common and vocal, the media--particularly print media--depended on government advertisements for a significant percentage of their revenue. Consequently, the media had an incentive for self-censorship.

The government in power, like its predecessors, issued new broadcast licenses to political supporters and denied them to political opponents.

The government did not subject foreign publications and films to stringent review and censorship. A government-managed film censorship board reviewed local and foreign films and had the authority to censor or ban films on the grounds of state security, law and order, religious sentiment, obscenity, foreign relations, defamation, or plagiarism, but was less strict than in the past. Video rental libraries and DVD shops stocked a wide variety of films, and government efforts to enforce censorship on rentals were sporadic and ineffective.

The government at times censored immodest or obscene photographs or objectionable comments regarding national leaders.

There were no significant government initiatives to foster media independence.

Internet Freedom

Individuals and groups generally engaged in the expression of views via the internet. The BTRC reported 438,000 active internet subscribers and 34,711,101 additional mobile internet subscribers. The BTRC filtered internet content the government deemed harmful to national unity and religious beliefs. The government also blocked some Facebook pages, including pages depicting the Prophet Muhammad and pages critical of both the prime minister and opposition leader. For example, BTRC Assistant Director Rahman Khan announced that his organization removed most of the posts from two blog platforms on April 4 for defaming Islam and the Prophet Mohammed days after police arrested four bloggers for their writings on those platforms. Bloggers and platform providers reported they received repeated requests from the NSI and DGFI to take down content.

The BTRC blocked Facebook and Twitter on February 28, citing technical reasons. The media claimed the block was to prevent the use of social media to organize protests following an ICT verdict. The BTRC unblocked both sites later that day. On June 5, the BTRC unblocked YouTube after blocking access in September 2012, following the posting of *The Innocence of Muslims* video.

The government has used the threat of sedition charges, which carry a possible death penalty, to limit online activity. For example, a Bangladeshi court recommended charging Muhammad Ruhul Khandaker with sedition for a comment he posted to his personal Facebook account while living in Australia. In January 2012 a court sentenced Khandaker in his absence to six months in jail for contempt of court when he failed to attend a hearing in Dhaka in relation to the comment, which was considered insulting to Prime Minister Sheikh Hasina. In October 2012 Australian immigration authorities granted Khandaker asylum.

On October 6, parliament amended the Information and Communication Technology Act to increase penalties for cybercrime, make more offenses ineligible for bail, and give law enforcement officers broader authority to arrest violators without a court order. Opponents of the law stated that section 57, which criminalizes the posting of inflammatory or derogatory information against the state or individuals online, stifles freedom of speech. At year's end the government had opened section 57 cases against bloggers Subrata Adhikari Shuvo, Russel Parvez, Mashiur Rahman Biplob, and Asif Mohiuddin; human rights activist Adilur Rahman Khan (see section 5); and journalist Mahmudur Rahman.

On October 8, authorities arrested A. K. M. Wahiduzzaman, a teacher at National University, on defamation charges for posting derogatory comments about the prime minister's children on his Facebook page on August 22. A Dhaka magistrate rejected his bail petition and sent him to jail on November 6. The case continued at year's end.

Academic Freedom and Cultural Events

The government had few restrictions on academic freedom or cultural events. Media groups reported that authorities discouraged research on sensitive religious and political topics that might fuel possible religious or communal tensions. Additionally, the Dhaka University teachers whom the government dismissed or put on extended leave after the AL-led government assumed office in 2009 remained outside the university. It was unclear whether authorities targeted the concerned teachers because of their political affiliations.

Academic publications on the Liberation War were also subject to scrutiny and government approval. On April 3, Minister for Planning A. K. Khandker came under scrutiny from the Prime Minister's Office for questioning the official account of the Liberation War. The minister considered resigning from the cabinet but ultimately did not.

b. Freedom of Peaceful Assembly and Association

The constitution provides for freedom of assembly and association, and the government generally respected these rights; however, there were instances of governmental action to limit freedom of assembly during periods of political protest and unrest.

Freedom of Assembly

The government permitted rallies, and they occurred with great regularity. On occasion, citing fear of violence, the government prevented political groups from holding meetings and demonstrations. For example, the government denied permission for the BNP to hold rallies on May 6 and 14. On October 19, police banned all rallies in Dhaka but gave permission for a BNP rally on October 25 and several other occasions. The law authorizes the government to ban assemblies of more than four persons. According to ASK, authorities used this provision at least 105 times from January through September. Occasionally, police or ruling party activists used force to disperse demonstrations.

On May 5 and 6, the government employed security agencies to disperse thousands of Hefazat-e-Islami supporters forcefully during their "siege of Dhaka" protests. While the government initially granted permission for Hefazat to hold the rally, officials ordered the Hefazat supporters to leave Motijheel Square after their rally turned violent. The demonstrators did not leave voluntarily, and the government claimed 11 persons died in ensuing clashes between police and the conservative Islamic group. Most news outlets on the scene maintained the number of fatalities ranged from 10 to 16, including security personnel. HRW and Al-Jazeera reported at least 50 deaths, and Odhikar, in a June report, maintained 61 persons died during the two-day period from a variety of causes (see section 5).

Jamaat reported that the government severely hampered its ability to secure permits for rallies or processions throughout the year. Government officials also prohibited Jamaat leaders from meeting at the party's headquarters.

Freedom of Association

The law provides for the right of citizens to form associations, subject to "reasonable restrictions" in the interest of morality or public order, and the government generally respected this right. Individuals were free to join private groups. In contrast to previous years, the government registered 54 garment sector trade unions as of October. The government's NGO Affairs Bureau sometimes withheld its approval for foreign funding to NGOs working in sensitive areas such as human rights, labor rights, indigenous rights, or humanitarian assistance to Rohingya refugees (see sections 2.d., 5, and 7). After three years the government approved a 2010 request of one international NGO to work in an official refugee camp to provide humanitarian assistance to Rohingya refugees. The government revoked the visa for another international NGO's resident nutritionist who worked on the same problem. There were reports of continued scrutiny of and restrictions on activities of NGOs by the NGO Affairs Bureau.

c. Freedom of Religion

See the Department of State's *International Religious Freedom Report* at www.state.gov/j/drl/irf/rpt/.

d. Freedom of Movement, Internally Displaced Persons, Protection of Refugees, and Stateless Persons

The law provides for freedom of movement within the country, foreign travel, emigration, and repatriation, and the government generally respected these rights, except in two sensitive areas, the CHT and Cox's Bazar.

The government did not fully cooperate with the UNHCR and other humanitarian organizations in providing protection and assistance to refugees, asylum seekers, stateless persons, and other persons of concern.

Foreign Travel: Passport holders do not require exit permits or visas to leave the country. There were no special controls on women or minorities. Some senior opposition officials reported extensive delays in getting their passports renewed. The international travel ban continued on war crimes suspects from the 1971 Liberation War.

The country's passports are invalid for travel to Israel.

Internally Displaced Persons (IDPs)

Low-level armed conflict in the CHT in the 1973-97 period displaced tens of thousands of indigenous persons internally. During the conflict the government relocated landless Bengalis from the plains with the unstated objective of changing the demographic balance in the CHT toward a Bengali majority.

The IDPs in the CHT had limited physical security. Indigenous community leaders maintained that settlers' violations of indigenous persons' rights, sometimes with the involvement of security forces, were widespread.

The IDPs in the CHT also lacked sufficient access to courts and legal aid. The CHT Commission, composed of experts from inside and outside the country who sought to promote respect for rights in the CHT, found that a lack of information and lawyers to assist indigenous persons hindered IDP access to justice. The CHT Commission reported that settlers expropriated indigenous land using false titles, intimidation, force, fraud, and manipulation of government eminent-domain claims (see section 6).

The number of IDPs in the CHT remained disputed. In 2000 a government task force estimated the number to be 500,000 but included nonindigenous persons in its estimate. An Amnesty International report published in June estimated 90,000 indigenous IDPs. The prime minister pledged to resolve outstanding land disputes in the CHT to facilitate the return of the IDPs and to close the remaining military camps. No land disputes were resolved during the year.

Protection of Refugees

The government and UNHCR provided temporary protection and basic assistance to approximately 30,000 Rohingya refugees from Burma living in two official camps (Kutupalong and Nayapara). The UNHCR estimated that an additional 200,000 undocumented Rohingya lived in the Cox's Bazar, Bandarban, and Chittagong districts, while the government estimated that 200,000 to 500,000 undocumented Rohingya resided during the year in various villages and towns outside the two official refugee camps. Most of these undocumented Rohingya lived among the local population in Teknaf and Ukhyia in Cox's Bazar District, including approximately 20,000 at an unofficial site adjacent to the official Kutupalong refugee camp and 9,000 at a site called Leda. Led by the Ministry of Foreign Affairs, the government developed a national strategy on Rohingya, but the government had not shared the policy with the international community by year's end.

Access to Asylum: The law does not provide for granting asylum or refugee status, nor has the government established a formal system for providing protection to refugees. The government provided some protection to Rohingya refugees from Burma already resident in the country, but it continued to deny asylum to the undocumented Rohingya whom it categorized as illegal economic migrants. While the government cooperated with the UNHCR in providing temporary protection and basic assistance to registered refugees already resident in two official camps, it did not cooperate with the UNHCR to expand services to undocumented Rohingya, who were persons of concern to the UNHCR, or to new arrivals fleeing violence in bordering Rakhine State, Burma. In June and October 2012, sectarian violence flared in Burma's northern Rakhine State, leading Bangladesh to close its borders and initially push fleeing asylum seekers back into Burma. Ultimately, during the crisis, it did allow the most vulnerable to cross and provided basic services. During the year the government reverted to its initial policy of pushing back Rohingya, and, as of the end of September, the UNHCR estimated the government returned more than 5,700 Rohingya to Burma.

Refoulement: Continued violence and human rights abuses against the Rohingya in Burma prevented the safe and voluntary return of refugees to their homes. Between January and September, according to the UNHCR, the Ministry of Foreign Affairs and Border Guard Bangladesh (BGB) forcibly turned back an estimated 5,700 Rohingya to Burma. According to the UNHCR, which maintained a field presence in both countries, many of these individuals were likely entitled to refugee status and protection. Despite these pushbacks the border remained porous, and the UNHCR acknowledged the existence of considerable daily cross-border movement for trade, smuggling, and illegal migration.

Refugee Abuse: The UNHCR reported cases of refugee abuse, including rape, assault, domestic violence, deprivation of food, arbitrary detention, and documentation problems.

Employment: The government did not allow Rohingya refugees living in the country to work locally. Refugees had limited freedom of movement beyond the camps and had to obtain permission for all movement outside the camps. Despite these constraints some refugees worked illegally as manual laborers or rickshaw pullers in the informal economy. Undocumented Rohingya also worked illegally, mostly in day-labor jobs.

Access to Basic Services: Working with the UNHCR the government continued to improve some aspects of the official refugee camps following findings in recent years that sanitation, nutrition, and shelter conditions had fallen below minimum international standards. Some basic standards remained unmet, and the camps remained overcrowded, with densities on par with the country's urban slums. A 2012 nutrition survey report from the UNHCR and World Food Program stated that the prevalence of malnourished (stunted) and underweight children in refugee camps remained higher than in the rest of the country and above the emergency threshold levels set by the World Health Organization.

Public education, while mandatory as of 2010 through eighth grade throughout the country, is only enforced through fifth grade and only offered through fifth grade in the camps. Government authorities did not allow refugees to attend school beyond fifth grade outside the camps; however, small numbers of students studied with the assistance of private tutors and participated in countrywide school examinations through the high school level. By law those undocumented, including Rohingya, were not allowed to attend public schools, but many did so.

Government authorities did not allow registered or unregistered Rohingya formal and regular access to public health care. Instead, the UNHCR and NGOs provided basic health services in the official camps to registered refugees. Although humanitarian assistance provided by NGOs served registered Rohingya refugees, undocumented Rohingya, and the local Bangladeshi population, the government's restrictions on NGO activities outside the camps limited the unregistered population's access to basic medical care and other services.

International NGOs faced difficulties in providing basic services to undocumented Rohingya and to the surrounding impoverished host communities due to extended delays by the NGO Affairs Bureau in granting permission for them to operate. By September the UNHCR's implementing NGO partners, Action against Hunger (ACF), Handicap International, and Solidarites International, were able to implement basic life-saving assistance. Three NGOs--Doctors without Borders , ACF, and Muslim Aid-UK--continued to provide basic assistance, such as water, sanitation, health care, and education, to unregistered Rohingya after receiving a cease-and-desist letter from the NGO Affairs Bureau in July 2012; however, they reduced their operations to provide only life-saving services.

Registered refugees did not have the right to legal recourse through the country's formal legal system, although they were able to take legal complaints to a local camp official, who could mediate disputes. The members of the unregistered population had no legal protection and were sometimes arrested because the government viewed them as illegal economic migrants.

Durable Solutions: Very few Rohingya voluntarily repatriated to Burma or resettled in third countries. Although there was no prospect of resolving the situation, the government did not facilitate local integration by conducting a census or considering any regularization of the Rohingya's status, such as naturalization. Government officials advised that the new Rohingya strategy recommended a "listing exercise" to identify all undocumented Rohingya in Cox's Bazar.

Stateless Persons

The Rohingya in the country are legally stateless. They cannot derive citizenship from birth in the country, marriage with local citizens, or any other means.

Section 3. Respect for Political Rights: The Right of Citizens to Change Their Government

The constitution provides citizens the right to change their government peacefully, and citizens exercised this right through periodic, free, and fair elections based on universal suffrage.

The Supreme Court's September 2012 decision abolishing temporary caretaker governments during elections continued to fuel a political impasse between the AL and the opposition BNP. This disagreement led to increased political violence, including attacks against civilians and children (see section 1.a.). Ballots prepared during the year for more than half of the parliamentary seats to be chosen in elections scheduled for January 5, 2014, contained only a single candidate.

Elections and Political Participation

Recent Elections: Sheikh Hasina, the leader of the AL, became prime minister in 2009 following the most recent parliamentary elections in 2008, which international and local observers deemed free and fair. The 14-party AL Alliance held 308 of the 350 seats in parliament. The opposition BNP and its allies held 41 seats. One seat belonged to an independent member. Sheikh Hasina's cabinet included representatives from the other parties in her coalition. BNP chairperson and former prime minister Khaleda Zia became leader of the opposition.

Political Parties: Opposition parties boycotted parliament throughout the year but returned during the budget session and on certain other days to fulfill requirements for them to retain their seats. Opposition parties participated in standing parliamentary committees despite their absence from parliament.

In some instances the government interfered with the right of opposition parties to organize public functions (see section 2.b.). It also manipulated the media to restrict the broadcasting of opposition political events (see section 2.a.).

On November 2, the Supreme Court's High Court Division published a full judgment reaffirming its earlier verdict cancelling the registration of Jamaat as a political party with the Election Commission. Jamaat's appeal of this decision continued at year's end.

Participation of Women and Minorities: There are no laws preventing women or minorities from voting or participating in political life. Women are eligible to contest any of the 300 directly elected seats in parliament, and an additional 50 seats are reserved for women. During the year there were 69 women in parliament, 19 directly elected and 50 chosen by political parties based on their proportional representation in parliament. Five women were full cabinet ministers, and three women served at the state ministerial level. Shirin Sharmin Chaudhury became the speaker of parliament on June 2.

There is no provision to reserve parliamentary seats for minorities.

Section 4. Corruption and Lack of Transparency in Government

The law provides criminal penalties for corruption by officials, but the government did not implement the law effectively. Human rights groups, the media, the Anticorruption Commission (ACC), and other institutions reported government corruption during the year. Officials frequently engaged in corrupt practices with impunity.

Corruption: The ACC is the government agency charged with fighting corruption. According to a 2010 World Bank report, the government undermined the ACC's work and hampered the prosecution of corruption. The report stated that the government filed far fewer corruption cases than the previous caretaker government and that a government commission recommended that the ACC drop thousands of corruption cases. Some in civil society stated that the government was not serious about fighting corruption and that the government used the ACC for politically motivated prosecutions. Transparency International Bangladesh asserted that political interference in the ACC's operations had rendered it a "toothless tiger." A November 10 amendment to the ACC Law removed the ACC's authority to sue public servants without prior government permission. Additionally, ACC inquiry officers may be sued and face two to five years in jail if they fail to prove their graft charges in court.

On January 31, the government withdrew its request for a 96 billion taka ($1.2 billion) loan from the World Bank for the Padma Bridge project. The decision followed criticism by a World Bank External Panel of International Experts of the ACC's failure to bring charges against former communications minister Syed Abul Hossain, based on what the panel believed was clear evidence of his role in a corruption scandal. On September 19, a foreign court brought formal charges against former state minister for foreign affairs Abul Hasan Chowdhury, who also was implicated in the affair.

The government took steps to address widespread police corruption. The inspector general of police continued to train police to address corruption and create a more responsive police force. No assessment of the training's effect on corruption within the police force was available.

The government subjected the judiciary to political pressure, and cases involving opposition leaders often proceeded in an irregular fashion.

Corruption remained a serious problem within the judiciary and was a factor in lengthy delays of trials, which were subjected to witness tampering and intimidation of victims. Several reports by human rights groups and corruption watchdog groups indicated growing public dissatisfaction with the perceived politicization of the judiciary.

Whistleblower Protection: The Public Interest Information Disclosure Act provides protection to public officials for making internal disclosures or lawful public disclosures of evidence of illegality, such as the solicitation of bribes or other corrupt acts, gross waste or fraud, gross mismanagement, abuse of power, and dangers to public health and safety. The law does not provide similar protection to private sector employees. The ACC reported in August 2012 that only 10 percent of government employees knew about the law. In addition to lack of awareness, the potential for two to five years in jail should the investigation prove the claimant knowingly presented false information might deter employees from filing claims.

Financial Disclosure: The laws do not require elected or appointed officials to disclose their income and assets. The AL promised in its election manifesto that ministers and members of parliament would disclose their assets, but they did not.

Public Access to Information: The law provides for public access to government information, but it was not fully effective. The Information Commission is responsible for implementing the law, which lists a few exceptions (due to national security) and establishes nominal processing fees. The commission has the authority to issue summons if individuals do not comply with a request for information and to compel them to give oral or written evidence under oath. Observers noted that the government filed few cases during the year due to limited understanding of the law and limited capacity to file and pursue requests for information. The commission conducted public outreach and training of public officials to encourage effective use of the law.

Section 5. Governmental Attitude Regarding International and Nongovernmental Investigation of Alleged Violations of Human Rights

A wide variety of domestic and international human rights groups generally operated independently and without government restriction, investigating and publishing their findings on human rights cases. Although human rights groups often sharply criticized the government, they also practiced some self-censorship. Government officials generally were not cooperative and responsive to their views.

UN and Other International Bodies: The government required all NGOs, including religious organizations, to register with the Ministry of Social Welfare (MSW). Local and international NGOs working on sensitive topics, such as human rights, indigenous people, Rohingya refugees, or worker rights, faced both formal and informal governmental restrictions. HRW, Odhikar, and international NGOs that provide assistance to Rohingya refugees reported numerous credible instances in which the government impeded their work, either by canceling projects or subjecting them to restrictive operating requirements that often resulted in a temporary or permanent cessation of their work. These groups also claimed that intelligence agencies monitored them. The government sometimes restricted international NGOs' ability to operate through delays in project registration, cease-and-desist letters, or visa refusals.

The government restricted the operations of Odhikar through the August 10 arrest and two-month detention of its secretary, Adilur Rahman Khan (see section 2.a.); the August 11 seizure of five computers from Odhikar's office; and the September 4 arrest warrant for the NGO's president, Nasiruddin Elan. These actions began after the June publication of Odhikar's report on the government's use of force during the May 5-6 Hefazat rally, which cited 61 deaths, higher than the government's figure of 11 (see section 2.b.). The government demanded Odhikar provide the names of those the NGO claimed died, but Odhikar refused to do so until the government furnished assurances of witness protection and agreed to investigate the events of May 5-6. The government determined the report was derogatory to the state and inflammatory, which led to Khan's arrest. Odhikar's staff in Dhaka and its network of volunteers in other districts reported additional harassment and claimed their telephone calls, e-mails, and movements were under constant surveillance by security officers. Odhikar failed to issue its monthly human rights monitoring reports during Khan's detention.

The government countered NGO criticism through the media, sometimes with intimidating or threatening remarks. On August 20, the ICT prosecution filed contempt of court charges against the HRW for asserting on June 16 that due process was not followed during the Ghulam Azam proceedings (see section 1.e.). HRW did not respond to the charges by the September 2 deadline, and the case remained open at year's end.

Government Human Rights Bodies: The National Human Rights Commission (NHRC) is a seven-member body, but five members are honorary. The NHRC has a small government support staff, but observers noted it was understaffed and underfunded. The NHRC's primary activity was educating the public about human rights, and the NHRC chairman made numerous media appearances. The International Coordinating Committee of National Institutions for the Promotion and Protection of Human Rights (ICC) found that the NHRC did not fully comply with international standards for such bodies. Specifically, the ICC focused on the lack of transparency in selecting NHRC commissioners and the NHRC's lack of hiring authority over its support staff.

Section 6. Discrimination, Societal Abuses, and Trafficking in Persons

The law specifically prohibits certain forms of discrimination against women, provides special procedures for persons accused of violence against women and children, calls for harsh penalties, provides compensation to victims, and requires action against investigating officers for negligence or willful failure of duty; however, enforcement was weak. Women, children, minority groups, persons with disabilities, indigenous people, and sexual minorities often confronted social and economic disadvantages.

Women

Rape and Domestic Violence: The law prohibits rape and physical spousal abuse but makes no specific provision for spousal rape. According to Odhikar from January through September, there were 729 reported incidents of rape against women and girls, including 305 women, 404 children, and 20 victims whose age could not be ascertained. Of the women, 55 were killed after being raped and 201 were victims of gang rape. ASK reported 702 rape cases, including 166 attempted rapes, filed with police during the first nine months of the year. Of the women, 69 were killed after being raped and 207 were victims of gang rape. Twelve women committed suicide after being raped. According to human rights monitors, the actual number of rape cases was higher because many rape victims did not report the incidents due to social stigma or fear of further harassment. Prosecution of rapists was weak and inconsistent. On January 13, Roich Sheikh raped a fifth-grade girl in Mulghor, Rajbari. Police had arrested Sheikh in June 2012 on attempted rape charges against the same girl but had released him on bail in December 2012.

The law criminalizes domestic violence. The government introduced a confidential hotline and opened several crisis centers for victims of domestic violence. Women's rights groups, however, criticized the government for its overall inaction on domestic violence, and data were difficult to obtain. From January through September, the Bangladesh National Women Lawyers' Association (BNWLA) received more than 2,569 reports of violence against women and filed 43 cases related to violence against women. NGOs, with little assistance from the government, funded most efforts to combat domestic violence. Courts sent most victims of domestic violence to shelter homes, such as those run by the BNWLA. In a few cases, the BNWLA sent victims to prison as a transitory destination for short periods. There were some support groups for victims of domestic violence.

A UN multi-agency study on violence against women, released on September 10, surveyed almost 2,400 men between the ages of 18 and 49 in one urban and one rural area of the country. According to the study, 55 percent of urban male respondents and 57 percent of rural respondents reported they themselves had perpetrated physical and/or sexual violence against women. The study concluded that the low prosecution rate of rapists supported a culture of impunity and encouraged further criminal acts of respondents who admitted to perpetrating rape. In total 88 percent of rural respondents and 95 percent of urban respondents reported they faced no legal consequences for rape charges.

Harmful Traditional Practices: Some NGOs reported violence against women was related to disputes over dowries. Odhikar reported 383 cases of dowry-related violence from January through September. Of this number, 125 cases involved victims who were killed and 15 involved victims who committed suicide. ASK reported 265 cases of dowry-related violence during the same period. Of this number, 128 cases involved victims who were killed and 21 involved victims who committed suicide. For example, 21- year-old Nilufa died on March 2 after her husband, Rakib Hossain, beat her in Sadar, Natore. Hossain told his in-laws that the model of motorcycle they gave him was not the one they had promised as part of Nilufa's dowry. Nilufa's family filed a case with the police against Rakib and his parents. The police completed their investigation, and court hearings continued at year's end.

On May 12, the Supreme Court's Appellate Division overruled a 2001 high court ruling prohibiting fatwas (religious edicts). In its ruling, however, the court declared that fatwas may be used only to settle religious matters and may not be invoked to justify meting out punishment, nor may they supersede existing secular law. Islamic tradition dictates that only those religious scholars with expertise in Islamic law may declare a fatwa. Despite these restrictions village religious leaders sometimes made such declarations. The declarations resulted in extrajudicial punishments, often against women, for perceived moral transgressions.

Incidents of vigilantism against women occurred, sometimes led by religious leaders enforcing fatwas. According to ASK there were 21 incidents of vigilante violence against women during the year, but only five incidents resulted in police action. The incidents included whipping, beating, and other forms of physical violence.

Acid attacks, although less common than in the past, remained a serious problem. Assailants threw acid in the faces of victims--usually women--leaving them disfigured and often blind. Acid attacks often related to a woman's refusal to accept a marriage proposal or to land disputes.

The Acid Survivors Foundation reported acid attacks on 31 women, 23 men, nine girls, and one boy from January through September. Odhikar reported acid attacks on 31 women, seven men, four girls, and two boys, and ASK reported acid attacks on 36 women. The law seeks to control the availability of acid and reduce acid-related violence directed toward women, but lack of awareness of the law and poor enforcement limited its effect. The government made efforts to punish offenders and reduce the availability of acid to the general public. The Commerce Ministry restricted acid sales to buyers registered with relevant trade organizations; however, the government did not enforce the restrictionsuniversally. The law provides for speedier prosecutions of acid-throwing cases in special tribunals and generally does not allow bail. According to the Acid Survivors Foundation, the special tribunals were not entirely effective, and conviction rates remained low. The Police Acid Crime Control Monitoring Cell stated prosecutors obtained a conviction in 10 percent of such cases from 2002 to March 2013. From January to September, courts convicted 10 persons in three cases.

Sexual Harassment: Sexual harassment in public and private, including in educational institutions and workplaces, is a criminal offense; however, harassment remained a problem and sometimes prevented girls from attending school or work. Odhikar reported 291 cases of harassment against women, and ASK reported 157, although many incidents went unreported. On June 5, a supervisor at Kachua Garments in Fatullah, Narayanganj, sexually harassed worker Khadiza Akhter Munni. Khadiza committed suicide on June 6.

Reproductive Rights: Couples and individuals had the information to decide the number, spacing, and timing of children free from discrimination, coercion, or violence through access to a full range of contraceptive methods, including long-acting reversible contraception and permanent methods. Pharmacies carried a wide range of family planning options and sold 41 percent of family planning supplies distributed. Low levels of income and education and traditional family roles often served as barriers to access, and most low-income families relied on public family planning services offered free of cost.

According to the 2010 Bangladesh Maternal Mortality Survey, the maternal mortality ratio declined by 40 percent during the preceding nine years, from 322 to 194 deaths per 100,000 live births. Approximately half of the maternal deaths were due to postpartum hemorrhage and eclampsia, with 7 percent attributed to obstructed or prolonged labor. According to the 2013 Utilization of Essential Service Delivery (UESD) survey, a skilled birth attendant delivered 34 percent of births, and 32.7 percent of the deliveries occurred at a health facility, compared with 31.7 and 29 percent, respectively, in 2011. Although 54.6 percent of women received at least one antenatal checkup from a medically trained provider, only 25.5 percent of women received the recommended four checkups following live births. Only 27 percent of the mothers received a postnatal checkup from a trained provider within two days of delivery.

Discrimination: Women do not enjoy the same legal status and rights as men in family, property, and inheritance law. Under traditional Islamic inheritance law, daughters inherit only half of what sons do, and in the absence of sons, they may inherit only what remains after settling all debts and other obligations. Under Hindu inheritance law, a widow's rights to her deceased husband's property are limited to her lifetime and revert to the male heirs upon her death.

Employment opportunities increased for women, who constituted approximately 80 percent of garment factory workers. Women were occasionally subjected to abuse in factories, including sexual harassment. There were some gender-based wage disparities in the overall economy, but wages of women and men were comparable in the garment sector. Women faced difficulty obtaining access to credit and other economic opportunities, but the government's National Women's Development Policy included commitments to provide opportunities for women in employment and business.

Children

Despite strong children's rights legislation, there is a general lack of enforcement due to limited resources and capacity to implement and monitor these laws. Governance remained weak, with the responsibility for children held by one of the least-resourced ministries, the Ministry of Women and Children's Affairs. On June 16, the government amended the Children's Act, raising the legal age of majority from 16 to 18 and adding extra protections for children from abuse. The government, with the assistance of local and foreign NGOs, worked to improve children's rights and welfare, enabling the country to make some progress in improving children's health, nutrition, and education. The 2013 UESD survey found that 38.7 percent of children remained chronically malnourished, as defined by moderate or severe levels of stunting (height for age). This was a decrease from 41.3 percent of stunting in 2011.

Birth Registration: The law does not grant citizenship automatically by birth within the country. Individuals become citizens if their fathers or grandfathers were born in the territories that are now part of the country. If a person qualifies for citizenship through ancestry, the father or grandfather must have been a permanent resident of these territories in or after 1971. The government began a universal birth registration program in 2005, which increased the registration rate from 10 percent to 51 percent by 2010.

Education: Primary education was free and compulsory through fifth grade, and the government offered subsidies to parents to keep girls in class through 10th grade. Teacher fees, books, and uniforms, however, were prohibitively costly for many families. While enrollments in primary schools showed gender parity, the percentage of girls declined in later secondary years. The 2010 Education Policy expanded the compulsory primary education from grades five to eight; however, until the government amends the law to reflect the new primary education period, the policy remained unenforceable. Government incentives to families that sent children to school contributed significantly to increased primary school enrollments in recent years, but hidden school fees at the local level created barriers to access for the poorest families. Many families kept children out of school to become wage earners or to help with household chores, and primary school coverage was insufficient in hard-to-reach and disaster-prone areas.

Child Abuse: All forms of child abuse, including sexual abuse, physical and humiliating punishment, child abandonment, kidnapping, and trafficking, continued to be serious and widespread problems. Children were vulnerable to abuse in all settings: home, community, school, residential institutions, and the workplace. Of the 729 officially reported incidents of rape against females, 404 were against girls. Of those child victims, 30 were killed after being raped, 83 were victims of gang rape, and three committed suicide after the crime. Local human rights groups reported numerous rapes and rape attempts against girls under age 17 during the year (see also section 1.c).

Despite advances, including establishing a monitoring agency in the MHA, trafficking of children and providing care and protection to survivors of trafficking continued to be problems. Child labor and abuse at the workplace remained problems in certain industries, mostly in the informal sector, and child workers were vulnerable to all forms of abuse at their informal workplaces.

Forced and Early Marriage: The legal age of marriage is 18 for women and 21 for men, but underage marriage was a widespread problem. Reliable statistics concerning underage marriage were difficult to identify because marriage and birth registrations were sporadic. The UN's *State of the World's Children 2013* report stated that, between 2002 and 2011, 66 percent of women between the ages of 20 and 24 were married by age 18 and 32 percent were married by age 15. In an effort to reduce child marriages, the government offered stipends for girls' school expenses beyond the compulsory fifth grade level. The government and NGOs conducted workshops and public events to teach parents the importance of waiting until their daughters were 18 to marry.

Sexual Exploitation of Children: The penalty for sexual exploitation of children is 10 years' to life imprisonment. The 2013 Children's Act defines a child as anyone under age 18. Child pornography, and the selling or distributing of such material, is prohibited. The Pornography Control Act sets the maximum penalty at 10 years in prison coupled with a fine of 500,000 taka ($6,250). In 2009, the most recent year for such data, the International Labour Organization (ILO) and Bangladesh Bureau of Statistics completed a baseline survey on commercial sexual exploitation of children. According to the survey, of 18,902 child victims of sexual exploitation, 83 percent were girls, 9 percent were transgender children, and 8 percent were boys. The survey reported that 40 percent of the girls and 53 percent of the boys were under age 16, the age of consent when the survey was conducted.

International Child Abductions: The country is not a party to the 1980 Hague Convention on the Civil Aspects of International Child Abduction. See country-specific information at http://travel.state.gov/content/childabduction/english/country/bangladesh.html.

Anti-Semitism

There was no Jewish community in the country, and there were no reports of anti-Semitic acts, but some newspapers occasionally printed anti-Semitic articles and commentary.

Trafficking in Persons

See the State Department's *Trafficking in Persons Report* at www.state.gov/j/tip/.

Persons with Disabilities

On October 3, parliament passed the Disability Rights and Protection Act, replacing the 2001 Disabled Persons Welfare Act. The amended law provides for equal treatment and freedom from discrimination for persons with disabilities; however, persons with disabilities faced social and economic discrimination. The law focuses on prevention of disability, treatment, education, rehabilitation, social protection, employment, transport accessibility, and advocacy.

The law requires persons with disabilities to register for identity cards to track their enrollment in educational institutions and access to jobs. Giving unequal treatment for school, work, or inheritance based on disability is punishable with fines up to 500,000 taka ($6,250) or three years' imprisonment. The law also created a 27-member National Coordination Committee charged with coordinating relevant activities among all government organizations and private bodies to fulfill the objectives of the law.

The NGO Action on Disability and Development estimated that there were 16 million persons with disabilities, or 10 percent of the population. The government estimated a lower figure of approximately 1.5 percent of the population.

According to the NGO Action against Disability, 90 percent of children with disabilities did not attend public school. The government trained teachers on inclusive education and recruited disability specialists at the district level. The government also allocated stipends for students with disabilities.

The law contains extensive accessibility requirements for new buildings. Authorities approved construction plans for new buildings without compliance with these requirements.

The law afforded persons with disabilities the same access to information rights as those without disabilities, but family and community dynamics often influenced whether or not these rights were exercised. The law contains provisions for information and communications technology to be accessible to persons with disabilities through video subtitling, sign language, screen readers, or text-to-speech systems in public and private media outlets. Some public television channels used sign language.

The law identifies persons with disabilities as a priority group for government-sponsored legal services. The MSW, Department of Social Services, and National Foundation for the Development of the Disabled are the government agencies responsible for protecting the rights of persons with disabilities. Due to inaccessibility and discrimination, persons with disabilities were sometimes excluded from mainstream government health, education, and social protective services. The government reduced taxes on several hundred items, such as wheelchairs, hearing aids, Braille machines, and orthotics and prostheses, designed to assist persons with disabilities.

Government facilities for treating persons with mental disabilities were inadequate. The Ministry of Health established child development centers in all public medical colleges to assess neurological disabilities. Several private initiatives existed for medical and vocational rehabilitation as well as for employment of persons with disabilities. National and international NGOs provided services and advocated for persons with disabilities. The government established service centers for persons with disabilities in all 64 districts, where local authorities provided free rehabilitation services and assistive devices. The government also promoted autism research and awareness. Parliament passed the Neuro-Development Disability Protection Trust Act 2013 on November 4.

National/Racial/Ethnic Minorities

Violent attacks against the Hindu minority community took place in 50 of 64 districts following the February 28 death sentence of Islamic leader Delwar Hossain Sayedee. The Hindu Buddhist Christian Unity Committee reported six deaths and 56 injuries as of September 24, with 142 temples, 262 houses, and 219 minority-owned businesses looted or burned. Religious sites and minority-owned homes and businesses in two Christian villages and one Buddhist village were also attacked. Local and international press, human rights organizations, and Hindu community leaders blamed the attacks on the Islami Chhatra Shibir, the student wing of the Jamaat party that Sayedee formerly had led. Authorities provided temporary accommodation to those made homeless. Victims sought remuneration for damages and asked law enforcement officials to strengthen protection for them and file criminal charges against the attackers. Authorities arrested six Jamaat supporters on March 3 in Kotalipara, and four Jamaat-Shibir men on March 11 in connection with attacks in Banshkhali and Sitakundu.

Indigenous People

The indigenous community experienced widespread discrimination and abuses, despite government quotas for indigenous participation from CHT residents in the civil service and higher education as called for in the 1997 Peace Accord. Indigenous persons from the CHT were unable to participate effectively in decisions affecting their lands due to disagreements regarding the structure and policies of the land commission. Strict security measures prevented some indigenous individuals and activists from combating discrimination.

Indigenous persons also suffered from societal violence. According to Odhikar, clashes between ethnic Bengali settlers and members of the indigenous community, as well as other forms of violence, led to 22 deaths, 18 injuries, and six rapes of indigenous people.

On April 4, a truck driver allegedly raped a 12-year-old indigenous Tripura domestic worker in Keranihat Village, Chittagong District. The Tripura Welfare Association of Bandarban gave the girl shelter for her safety and began preparing a written statement against her attacker to file with the local police.

Extensive societal violence against indigenous individuals occurred on August 3 in six villages in the Taindong area of Matiranga, Kagrachari, after rumors spread that indigenous persons had kidnapped a Bengali motorcyclist. Retaliatory attacks against members of these communities caused more than 2,000 indigenous families to flee across the border to Tripura, India, and resulted in 12 injuries, 34 burned houses, two damaged Buddhist temples, and 259 looted homes. Locals reported the BGB stationed nearby did not take adequate steps to prevent the attacks or to stop them after they began. Authorities ultimately arrested 11 persons in connection with the attacks, including the motorcyclist who faked his own kidnapping, but they were free on bail at year's end.

Criminal proceedings began against 19 of the 540 individuals arrested in connection with the October 2012 destruction of Buddhist religious sites around

Ramu. While the prosecution charged suspects in seven cases, the courts did not convict any individuals or issue any sentences. Local religious leaders stated authorities shielded those affiliated with the AL from criminal prosecution. Suspects identified in the official administrative and judicial inquiries remained free.

Indigenous groups and NGOs reported increased monitoring by civilian and military intelligence agencies. The CHT Commission did not conduct its annual reporting missions in the three hill tracts divisions in 2012 or during the year due to its inability to conduct private meetings with local partners in 2011.

The central government retained authority over land use. The land commission, designed to investigate and return all illegally acquired land, did not resolve any disputes throughout the year, as Bengalis and indigenous persons questioned the structure and impartiality of the commission.

Indigenous communities in areas other than the Hill Tracts reported the loss of land to Bengali Muslims. The government continued construction projects on land traditionally owned by indigenous communities in the Moulvibazar and Modhupur forest areas but did not undertake any new activities. Indigenous communities, local human rights organizations, and churches in those areas claimed the government had not withdrawn thousands of false charges that the Forestry Department had filed against indigenous residents.

Societal Abuses, Discrimination, and Acts of Violence Based on Sexual Orientation and Gender Identity

Consensual same-sex sexual activity is illegal, but the law was not enforced. Lesbian, gay, bisexual, and transgender (LGBT) groups reported police used the law as a pretext to bully LGBT individuals, particularly those seen as effeminate men. The government acknowledged the existence of the LGBT population during its April Universal Periodic Review, contrary to its stance in the 2009 review during which the foreign minister stated there were no LGBT individuals in the country. Additionally, the government allocated funds for the transgender and hijra (transgender) population in the national budget.

On November 11, the government announced it would consider hijras, who numbered approximately 10,000 according to an MSW survey, as a separate gender, neither male nor female.

There were several informal support networks for gays, but organizations to assist lesbians were rare.

Attacks on LGBT persons occurred occasionally, but those offenses were difficult to document because victims desired confidentiality. The Bandhu Social Welfare Society, a local NGO, reported 69 cases of assault against LGBT persons from January through September, as compared with 137 in all of 2012. Strong social stigma based on sexual orientation was common and prevented open discussion of the subject.

Other Societal Violence or Discrimination

Vigilante killings occurred during the year. Odhikar reported at least 100 killings through mob justice, and ASK reported at least 99, but local human rights organizations acknowledged that the number of reported cases probably represented only a fraction of the actual incidents. One prominent case occurred on June 14, when locals from Subarnochar, Noakhali, killed 10 members of a criminal gang. Locals reportedly heard the gang was at a village market planning to commit a robbery, chased them down, and beat them to death.

Illegal fatwas and village arbitration, which Odhikar defined as rulings given by community leaders rather than religious scholars, also occurred. Odhikar reported nine such cases throughout the year against both men and women, whereas ASK reported 21 such cases throughout the year against women, resulting sometimes in physical abuse. On June 27, local arbitrators, including government officials and teachers, beat a woman named Alomati, then seven months pregnant, 100 times and fined her 15,000 taka ($190) for entering into a marriage of which they did not approve.

There were no reported cases of violence or discrimination against HIV/AIDS patients. NGOs believed this was partly a function of the refusal of victims to identify themselves and an absence of research due to the relatively low rate of HIV/AIDS in the country.

Section 7. Worker Rights

a. Freedom of Association and the Right to Collective Bargaining

The law provides for the protection of the right to join unions and, with government approval, the right to form a union, although numerous restrictions on union registration remained. For example, the law requires a minimum of 30 percent of an enterprise's total workforce to agree to be members before the Ministry of Labor and Employment (MOLE) may grant approval for a union, and the MOLE may dissolve the union if membership falls below 30 percent. Managerial staff, firefighting staff, security guards, and other employees designated by employers as "confidential" may not join a union. Civil service and security force employees are prohibited from forming unions. The registrar of trade unions may deregister unions with the approval of a labor court. The law affords unions the right of appeal in the cases of dissolution or denial of registration.

The law provides for the right to conduct legal strikes but with many limitations. For example, the government may prohibit at any time a strike deemed to pose a "serious hardship to the community" and may terminate any strike lasting more than 30 days. The law additionally prohibits strikes for the first three years of commercial production or if the factory was built with foreign investment or owned by a foreign investor.

Legally registered unions are entitled to bargain collectively with employers; however, this rarely occurred. Labor organizations reported that in some companies workers did not exercise their collective bargaining rights due to their unions' ability to address grievances with management informally or due to fear of reprisal.

The law includes provisions protecting unions from employer interference in organizing activities; however, employers, particularly in the ready-made garment industry, often sought to curtail this right. Amendments to the labor law in July require every factory of more than 50 employees to have an elected participation committee, but by year's end the MOLE had not drafted the regulations necessary to implement the requirement.

A separate legal framework under the authority of the Bangladesh Export Processing Zone (EPZ) Authority (BEPZA) governs labor rights in the country's EPZs. EPZ factory officials interpreted EPZ regulations and applicable law narrowly and claimed they were exempted from broader labor law. EPZ law specifies certain limited associational and bargaining rights for elected worker welfare associations, such as the rights to bargain collectively and represent their members in disputes. While the EPZ law provision banning all strikes under penalty of imprisonment expired on October 31, the law continues to provide for strict limits on the right to strike, such as the discretion of the BEPZA chairman to ban any strike he views as prejudicial to the public interest. The law provides for EPZ labor tribunals, appellate tribunals, and conciliators, but those institutions have not been established. Worker associations are also prohibited from establishing any connection to outside political parties, unions, or NGOs.

With the exception of the limited associational rights and worker protections in the EPZs, national labor law prohibits anti-union discrimination. Union activists noted that the MOLE shared lists of union supporters with enterprises, as required by law, leading to anti-union firings. The law was amended during the year to remove this requirement. A labor court may order the reinstatement of workers fired for union activities.

The government did not always enforce applicable law effectively. For example, the Bangladesh Labor Act establishes mechanisms for conciliation, arbitration, and dispute resolution by a labor court. Civil servants and security forces are covered under different terms and conditions of employment and file cases in specified courts, such as an administrative tribunal. Workers in a collective-bargaining union have the right to strike in the event of a failure to reach a settlement. In practical terms few strikes followed the cumbersome legal requirements, and strikes or walkouts often occurred spontaneously. Resources at the MOLE were inadequate to inspect and remediate problems effectively. Penalties for violating the law were not sufficient to deter violations. Administrative and judicial appeals were subjected to lengthy delays.

Unlike in previous years, the MOLE formally investigated complaints of unfair union discrimination. For example, the MOLE investigated a complaint at Rebeka Fashions and issued a finding supporting union allegations.

Odhikar reported that between January and September, employers terminated 1,405 garment workers for demanding increased wages.

Law enforcement officials confronted factory workers in the garment industry who held protests to demand increased wages. On September 21, garment workers attended a rally organized by Shipping Minister Shahjahan Khan. Wage protests began almost immediately thereafter, resulting in more than 70 injuries and causing more than 160 factories to close in Savar, Ashulia, and Gazipur. On November 4, a government-appointed minimum wage board voted to raise the minimum wage in the garment industry from 3,000 taka ($37.50) per month to 5,300 taka ($66.25).

Labor organizers reported acts of intimidation and abuse, the firing of employees, and increased scrutiny by security forces and the NSI. Labor rights NGOs alleged that some terminated union members were unable to find work in the sector because employers blacklisted them. The American Center for International Labor Solidarity (Solidarity Center) reported that, of 66 unions registered through November, nine experienced antiunion activities.

Workers applied to register a union at garment factory Rebeka Fashions in Kafrul, Dhaka, in December 2012. Four members of the union's board stated they were beaten, and management told them to cease their organizing activities. Although the MOLE approved their union's registration, the union's board members stated employers harassed them and forced them to resign. The MOLE viewed the workers' terminations as unlawful and ordered their reinstatement, but the factory owner did not rehire them. On July 29, the Bangladesh Garment Manufacturers and Exporters Association (BGMEA) brokered an agreement with the union to pay back wages and stop harassment. The union's president returned to work, but management relegated him to an isolated workspace and did not allow him to speak with other workers or conduct union activities. The factory closed on September 15.

Workers at Sadia Garments in Dhaka formed a union on February 24, and the MOLE approved their registration application on May 16. On May 27, management threatened the union members with physical violence, forcing union members to sign statements stating they would terminate their union. The BGMEA attempted to broker an agreement to stop management harassment, but when the workers returned to the factory, management beat the union members and threatened them with death unless they stopped their organizing activities. Employers forced workers to sign resignation letters. When the BGMEA again brokered an arrangement for the union members to return to work and for management to stop harassment, factory management hired outsiders to beat the union's general secretary, Maksuda, and five other union members with cutting floor shears. Management forced Maksuda to announce her resignation on the factory floor, and she was dismissed. Management also forced most of the union committee members to sign resignation papers. The terminated union members did not pursue legal action against Sadia management but reached a settlement and found other jobs. Sadia Garments management sponsored another union, which was registered in July.

The MHA in July ordered the deputy commissioner of Dhaka Division to ask the public prosecutor to drop outstanding criminal charges in 16 cases against leaders of the labor rights NGO Bangladesh Center for Workers Solidarity (BCWS) and the labor union federation Bangladesh Garment and Industrial Workers Federation (BGIWF) for their alleged participation in 2010 wage demonstrations. The courts had dropped seven of the eight remaining cases at year's end and were no longer actively pursuing the remaining open case. The MSW and the NGO Affairs Bureau reregistered the BCWS on August 13 and 19, respectively. The MSW withdrew a notice of pending deregistration against the shrimp sector NGO Social Activities for the Environment (SAFE), but by year's end the NGO Affairs Bureau had not registered SAFE after its April application.

No progress was made in the investigation of the April 2012 killing of Aminul Islam, an organizer for the BGIWF and a BCWS staff member.

b. Prohibition of Forced or Compulsory Labor

The law prohibits all forms of forced or compulsory labor; however, the prescribed penalty of imprisonment for up to one year or a fine was not sufficiently stringent to deter violations, and the government did not enforce the law effectively. The law does not include a specific prohibition of fraudulent recruitment, but it cites the concept of fraud as a possible element of human trafficking. Inspection mechanisms that enforce laws against forced labor did not function effectively. Resources, inspections, and remediation efforts were inadequate. Traffickers are subject to life imprisonment plus a fine of 500,000 taka ($6,250). The law also provides that victims of forced labor have access to shelter and other protective services afforded to trafficking victims.

Some individuals recruited to work overseas with fraudulent employment offers subsequently were exploited abroad under conditions of forced labor or debt bondage.

Although relatively uncommon in urban areas, there were instances of bonded labor in rural areas and domestic service. Children and adults were forced into domestic servitude and bonded labor that involved restricted movement, nonpayment of wages, threats, and physical or sexual abuse (see section 7.c.).

See the Department of State's *Trafficking in Persons Report* at www.state.gov/j/tip/.

c. Prohibition of Child Labor and Minimum Age for Employment

The law regulates child employment, depending on the type of work and the child's age. The minimum age for work is 14, and the minimum age for hazardous work is 18. The law allows for certain exceptions, permitting children who are ages 12 or 13 to perform restricted forms of light work. By law every child must attend school through fifth grade; July amendments to the Bangladesh Labor Act further restrict adolescents' work in hazardous areas.

The MOLE's enforcement mechanisms were insufficient for the large, urban informal sector, and there was little enforcement of child labor laws outside the export garment and shrimp-processing sectors. Agriculture and other informal sectors that had no government oversight employed large numbers of children.

The Child Labor Unit in the MOLE monitored, coordinated, and supervised child labor programs. Under the MOLE's Child Labor National Plan of Action, the National Child Labor Welfare Council is charged with monitoring child labor at district and subdistrict levels. In December 2012 the government approved Child Protection Networks at district and subdistrict levels. These networks were mandated to respond to a broad spectrum of violations against children, including child labor; monitor interventions; and develop referral mechanisms.

The government also developed a national program to eliminate the worst forms of child labor by 2015. The program includes monitoring workplaces and education for children and their families. The law specifies penalties for child labor violations, typically nominal fines of less than 5,000 taka ($62.50). These penalties were insufficient to deter violations. The government occasionally brought criminal charges against employers who abused domestic servants, but generally resources, inspections, and remedial action were inadequate.

Child labor was widespread, particularly in the informal sector and in domestic work. The ILO estimated that 3.7 million children worked and that 1.3 million worked in hazardous sectors. Children are engaged in the worst forms of child labor, primarily in dangerous activities in agriculture. Children working in agriculture risked using dangerous tools, carrying heavy loads, and applying harmful pesticides. Children frequently worked long hours, were exposed to extreme temperatures, and suffered high rates of injury from sharp tools. Children also worked in such hazardous activities as stone breaking, dyeing operations, blacksmith assistance, and construction. Forced child labor was present in the fish-drying industry, which exposed them to harmful chemicals, dangerous machines, and long hours of work. In urban areas street children engaged in work, such as begging, working as porters, shining shoes, collecting paper, and selling flowers.

These children were vulnerable to exploitation, for example, being used to smuggle or sell drugs.

Children frequently worked in the informal sector in areas including the garment, road transport, manufacturing, and service industries. An August 2012 survey of the unregistered garment sector in Dhaka, by the consulting firm ICF International, found that approximately one-third of workers were under age 18. The children in the survey reported they worked an average of six days a week for 10.5 hours a day. Undercover reporters filmed 12-year-old workers at Samie's Finishing House who were making finishing touches to Old Navy jeans. Old Navy's parent company, Gap, Inc., investigated the allegations and stated it had not placed any orders with the factory. Gap, Inc. officials stated that the jeans had not passed quality inspections at its supplier factory, which had sold them illegally to Samie's Finishing House.

See the Department of Labor's *Findings on the Worst Forms of Child Labor* at www.dol.gov/ilab/programs/ocft/tda.htm.

d. Acceptable Conditions of Work

The National Minimum Wage Board (NMWB) established the minimum monthly wage at 1,500 taka ($18.75) for all economic sectors not covered by industry-specific wages. The NMWB may convene at any time, but it must meet every five years in a tripartite forum to set wage structures and benefits industry by industry. Amendments to the Bangladesh Labor Act in July added language that the government may modify or amend existing wage structures through official public announcement in consultation with employers and workers. In the garment industry, the board raised the minimum monthly wage from 3,000 taka ($37.50) to 5,300 taka ($66.25). Wages in the apparel sector often were higher than the minimum wage, and wages in the EPZs were typically higher than general wage levels. None of the set minimum wages provided a sufficient standard of living for urban dwellers. The Center for Policy Dialogue, an independent think tank, reported a monthly wage of 6,500 taka ($81.25) was reasonable to cover living expenses. There was no mechanism to keep the minimum wage in line with inflation, which averaged 10 percent annually.

By law a standard workday is eight hours. A standard workweek is 48 hours but may be extended to 60 hours, subject to the payment of an overtime allowance that is double the basic wage. Workers must have one hour of rest if they work for more than eight hours a day or a half-hour of rest for more than five hours' work a day. Factory workers receive one day off every week. Shop workers receive one-and-a-half days off per week. The law establishes occupational health and safety standards, and amendments to the law during the year created mandatory worker safety committees.

The government did not effectively enforce minimum wage, hours of work, and occupational safety and health standards in all sectors. Resources, inspections, and remediation were not adequate, and penalties for violations were not sufficient to deter violations.

Workers' groups stated that the occupational safety and health standards established by law were sufficient, but that they were not routinely enforced. Workers may invoke legal mechanisms to enforce the law but did so in few cases. Enforcement by the MOLE's industrial inspectors was weak due to the low number of labor inspectors. There were 95 inspectors nationwide, of whom approximately 56 worked in the factories division. Inspections were supposed to be unannounced, but inspectors sometimes notified factory owners of coming inspections. The law provides for a maximum fine of 25,000 taka ($310) for noncompliance, but this did not deter violations. In contrast to previous years, when issuing violation notices was not customary, from February through September, official government factory inspectors issued violation notices to 305 garment factories for noncompliance with fire safety standards.

Legal limits on hours of work were violated routinely. In the ready-made garment sector, employers often required workers to labor 12 hours a day or more to meet export deadlines, but they did not always properly compensate workers for their time. Employers commonly delayed workers' pay or denied full leave benefits. Workers at Ha-Meem Group's sportswear factory told journalists they worked 19-hour shifts eight times during a two-week period, but management maintained its workers did not work in excess of 10 hours a day and were compensated for overtime. Next Collections, Ltd., another of Ha-Meem Group's factories, kept two sets of time sheets: official, electronic pay sheets for inspections and foreign buyers showed a 48-hour workweek with no more than 12 additional hours of overtime. Handwritten pay sheets, however, by which workers stated they were paid, showed employees regularly worked 14 hours a day and sometimes up to 20 hours to meet buyers' deadlines.

Safety conditions at many workplaces were extremely poor. Because of high unemployment rates and inadequate law enforcement, workers who demanded redress for dangerous working conditions or who refused to work under hazardous conditions risked losing their jobs. Factory fires continued throughout the year, with the Solidarity Center reporting 32 incidents. Many workers were injured or killed because of smoke inhalation, jumping from factory windows, or being trampled while trying to exit factories. Two of the deadliest factory fires during the year were at Smart Garments on January 27 and Aswad Composite Mills on October 8. Each of the fires killed at least seven workers.

On April 23, workers at five garment factories, a bank, and several retail stores in the nine-story Rana Plaza building in Savar noticed cracks in the walls and informed management. Industrial police and the BGMEA advised factory owners not to allow employees in the building until the authorities could conduct a proper structural assessment. On April 24, garment factory managers threatened to withhold workers' pay if they did not enter the building. The building collapsed, killing 1,133 workers and injuring more than 2,500. Rana Plaza was in violation of building codes and was only authorized for five stories of retail and commercial-- not industrial--space. The Dhaka city development authority filed a case against the building's owner, Sohel Rana, and the five garment factory owners on April 25 for criminal negligence and violation of the building code. Authorities arrested Rana on April 29, and he remained in jail at year's end. On June 10, seven inspectors were suspended and accused of negligence for renewing the licenses of the five garment factories. Hundreds of former workers and relatives of the deceased awaited back pay and compensation at year's end.

The owner of Tazreen Fashions, where a November 2012 fire killed 112 workers, remained free on bail while the police investigation continued. By year's end charges had been pressed against 13 persons related to worker deaths. The Supreme Court's High Court Division reported difficulty in obtaining timely reports from government authorities and the BGMEA that would enable the judges to conduct their work.

No reliable labor statistics were available on the large informal sector in which the majority of citizens worked, and it was difficult to enforce labor laws in the sector. The ILO reported that 47.3 million of the 56.7 million workers in the country were employed in the informal sector.

www.ingramcontent.com/pod-product-compliance
Lightning Source LLC
Chambersburg PA
CBHW080628290526
45790CB00007B/2973